HIP-HOP INSIDER

THE **WOMEN** OF
HIP-HOP

By Sheila Llanas

CONTENT CONSULTANT

RACHEL RAIMIST, PHD
ASSOCIATE PROFESSOR
DEPARTMENT OF JOURNALISM & CREATIVE MEDIA
UNIVERSITY OF ALABAMA

Essential Library

An Imprint of Abdo Publishing | abdopublishing.com

Printed in the United States of America, North Mankato, Minnesota
042017
092017

 **THIS BOOK CONTAINS RECYCLED MATERIALS**

Cover Photo: Jeff Lombardo/Invions/AP Images
Interior Photos: Reed Saxon/AP Images, 5; Kevork Djansezian/AP Images, 6–7, 8; Eddy Risch/Keystone/AP Images, 10; Henny Ray Abrams/AP Images, 15; Epic Stock Media/Shutterstock Images, 17; Richard B. Levine/Newscom, 20–21; Michael Ochs Archives/Getty Images, 25, 29; Gilbert Carrasquillo/WireImage/Getty Images, 27; Orion Pictures/Photofest NYC, 30–31; David Corio/Michael Ochs Archives/Getty Images, 33; Mark J. Terrill/AP Images, 35, 58–59; Jeff Kravitz/Film Magic, Inc/Getty Images, 41; Fred Prouser/Reuters/Newscom, 43; Jason Kempin/Getty Images Entertainment/Getty Images, 45; FS2 WENN Photos/Newscom, 47; Everett Collection/Shutterstock Images, 53, 67; Brad Barket/Invision/AP Images, 55; Joe Fudge/The Daily Press/AP Images, 61; Chris Martinez/La Opinion Photos/Newscom, 63; M. Caulfield/WireImage/Getty Images, 65; Featureflash Photo Agency/Shutterstock Images, 69; Ron Edmonds/AP Images, 70–71; Press Association/URN:28430555/AP Images, 74; Owen Sweeney/Invision/AP Images, 77; Amy Nichole Harris/Shutterstock Images, 79; Terrence Jennings/Polaris/Newscom, 83; MWK/BSK/EXP1/Wennchella/Wenn/Newscom, 84; Greg Allen/Invision/AP Images, 87; Dawn Villella/AP Images, 89; Jason Squires/WireImage/Getty Images, 90; DS7 Wenn Photos/Newscom, 92; Alex J. Berliner/ABImages/AP Images, 96

Editor: Jenna Trnka
Series Designer: Jake Nordby

Publisher's Cataloging-in-Publication Data
Names: Llanas, Sheila, author.
Title: The women of hip-hop / by Sheila Llanas.
Description: Minneapolis, MN : Abdo Publishing, 2018. | Series: Hip-hop insider | Includes bibliographical references and index.
Identifiers: LCCN 2016962258 | ISBN 9781532110320 (lib. bdg.) | ISBN 9781680788174 (ebook)
Subjects: LCSH: Hip-hop--Juvenile literature. | Rap musicians--Juvenile literature.
Classification: DDC 782--dc23
LC record available at http://lccn.loc.gov/2016962258

CONTENTS

1 LAURYN HILL'S NIGHT

Fans anticipated the 41st Annual Grammy Awards ceremony would be a big night for women. On that night, February 24, 1999, musicians gathered at the Shrine Auditorium in Los Angeles, California. Lauryn Hill had been nominated in ten categories for her album *The Miseducation of Lauryn Hill*. No female musician in any genre had ever received as many nominations in one year. No hip-hop record had ever before won the Grammys' biggest award: Album of the Year.

Céline Dion won Record of the Year for her pop hit "My Heart Will Go On" from the *Titanic* soundtrack. Madonna won Best Pop Album for *Ray of Light*. Alanis Morissette won Best Rock

Hill showcases her five Grammys after the 41st Annual Grammy

Song for "Uninvited," and Shania Twain and the Dixie Chicks won country music awards. It was hip-hop artist Hill, however, who stole the show. As the evening progressed, she won gold-plated statues for Best New Artist, Best Rhythm and Blues (R&B) Song for "Doo Wop (That Thing)," Best Female R&B Vocal Performance, and Best R&B Album.

Finally, Whitney Houston and Sting appeared onstage to announce the Grammys' most esteemed award: Album of the Year. Hill was up against rock albums *The Globe Sessions* by Sheryl Crow and *Version 2.0* by Garbage, Madonna's pop album *Ray of Light*, and Shania Twain's country album *Come on Over*. When *The Miseducation of Lauryn Hill* was announced the winner, everyone knew it was a historic

Hill pumps her first in the air in celebration after winning Best New Artist.

Hill dons a look of shock as presenter Whitney Houston hugs and congratulates her.

moment. It was a historic moment for hip-hop, for African Americans, and for women. Hill was the first woman to win five Grammys in one night. Her album was the first hip-hop record to ever win Album of the Year.

Going Solo

Similar to so many hip-hop artists, Hill entered the music industry as a teenager. Born in 1975 in South Orange, New

Jersey, Hill recorded with the Fugees. They released albums in 1994 and 1996. Their hit record, *The Score*, sold 17 million copies worldwide and brought Hill fame and fortune.[1] At that point, Hill, a 22-year-old new mother, decided to make a solo album. During this recording period, becoming pregnant did not deter her. Instead, Hill said expecting her second child only fueled her creativity. In her lyrics, she was not afraid to reveal her human frailty and her personal life or admit she made mistakes.

> "Every time I got hurt, every time I was disappointed, every time I learned, I just wrote a song."[2]
>
> —*Lauryn Hill*

Stylistically, Hill had a specific sound in mind for her solo album. Rather than electronically overproducing the music, Hill wanted a raw, muddy sound. She wanted it to sound real. She layered distinct musical styles, mixing rap with soul and R&B. By using older musical styles in a new way and by writing heartfelt, soul-baring lyrics, she led other hip-hop artists into the new millennium. Her raw musical styles would go on to inspire musicians such as Beyoncé and Adele. Hill even penned lyrics for musical icon Aretha Franklin, lending her new sound to the song "A Rose Is Still a Rose."

The Impact

The Miseducation of Lauryn Hill took everyone by surprise. Hill had delved deep into aspects of her personal life to write it. Her songs, both heartbreaking and uplifting, had

In 2005, Hill reunited with Fugees members Wyclef Jean, *left*, and Prakazrel "Pras" Michél, *right*, for a concert in Switzerland.

universal appeal. When the album dropped in August 1998, it broke the record for best-selling debut week for a female artist, selling one million copies in its first month alone. It has sold eight million copies in the United States.[3] After Hill's Grammy wins, the album's sales skyrocketed.

HILL'S DOO-WOP SOUND

To make the doo-wop sound in the 1950s, vocal groups sang in harmony in songs such as "Only You" by the Platters in 1955 and "Blue Moon" by the Marcels in 1961. Hill updated the doo-wop sound with hip-hop for the hit song "Doo Wop (That Thing)." With background singers creating melodic Motown harmonies, she laid down rap lyrics cautioning women against unreliable men.

The Miseducation of Lauryn Hill was a game changer. Released in the late 1990s, a tumultuous time in hip-hop, her intensely personal album seemed to launch a new era. "Hill is one of the performers set to take hip-hop into the new millennium," wrote one reviewer.[4] Fans and journalists anticipated more from her, expecting her career to reach megastardom. But over the course of the next few years, Hill disappeared from sight. She retreated into her private life.

At the same time, another rapper steadily grew her career. Beginning with her 1997 debut album, *Supa Dupa Fly*, Missy Elliott rose to become one of the biggest

LEAVING THE SCENE

When expectations for more music were not met, Hill was criticized for disappearing from the public eye. Reviewers speculated about why she left music. They reported she was mentally and emotionally unstable, even crazy. Perhaps Hill simply found her status as a celebrity overwhelming. Perhaps she wanted to raise her children with her partner Rohan Marley, son of reggae star Bob Marley. "I had created this public persona, this public illusion, and it held me hostage," Hill said. "I couldn't be a real person, because you're too afraid of what your public will say. At that point, I had to do some dying."[5]

rappers of all time—not the biggest female rapper but the biggest rapper, male or female. Hill and Elliott, as peers, having recorded music during the same era, created very different sounds. Hill's music is personal. Elliott's music is about performance and creating personas. In contrast to Hill's authentic and muddy old-music sound, Elliott's digitally synthesized music has a pronounced beat, a techno quality, and quirky lyrics. The images she describes in her lyrics resemble science fiction. Their differences in style illustrated that rap, in hip-hop culture, did not have to be limited.

In its 20-year history, hip-hop had fractured into subgenres, each with a distinct label. Crunk, turntablism, trip-hop, G-funk, reggaeton, acid rap, message rap, and horrorcore were just a few. Hip-hop was and is a male-dominated field, but throughout its evolution, women such as Hill and Elliott have broken through and made their mark. By the late 1990s, hip-hop had come a long way. But it still had a long way to go.

A SHORT-LIVED GRAMMY CATEGORY

In 1995, Queen Latifah became the first woman to win a Grammy for Best Rap Solo Performance for her song "U.N.I.T.Y." In 2002, Missy Elliott became the second. In 2003, the category was split into two awards, Best Male and Best Female Rap Solo Performance. Elliott won that year for her song "Scream a.k.a. Itchin'." She also won in 2004 for her hit "Work It." Winning three years in a row, Elliott took the category more often than any other rapper other than Eminem, who has won four times. Suddenly, in 2005, the award was restored to Best Rap Solo Performance. Grammy spokespeople said there were not enough female artists to justify dividing genders. During its two-year life-span, the category recognized talents such as Eve, Foxy Brown, Da Brat, and Lil' Kim.

2 FOUNDERS OF HIP-HOP

In New York City in the mid-1970s, crime, violence, drug use, unemployment, and poverty levels were high. The Bronx borough was particularly troubled. Street gangs thrived. Community members were desperate to keep teenagers off the streets and out of trouble. To do so, DJs played block parties. Bronx residents gathered to dance and blow off steam. These parties gave everyone something fun and creative to do. From these parties, hip-hop culture emerged. With its vibrant energy, hip-hop was a powerful vehicle of expression for urban African-American youth. It was a positive force during a dark time.

Afrika Bambaataa grew up in the South Bronx and helped develop and

At the time, disco was very popular. Rock and roll was still a radio standard. Punk rock was on the rise. Hip-hop was new and inventive. The culture of hip-hop included music, dance, and art. One of hip-hop's founders, Afrika Bambaataa, established four principles to empower the culture: "Peace, Unity, Love, and Having Fun."[1] Four specific art forms came to be associated with hip-hop: deejaying, emceeing, break dancing (b-boys and b-girls), and graffiti art. Break dancers responded to the hip-hop music by creating exciting new dance moves. Using spray paint, graffiti artists created bold and visual art styles.

A couple of hip-hop's first DJs were Kool Herc and Grandmaster Flash. When they played records, they found the breaks, or the places in songs that had no vocals or lyrics. Song breaks had pure, strong beats made with drum solos and bass guitar riffs. DJs would play those parts of a song over and over. To quickly find the breaks, they rubbed the record player's needle back and forth on the vinyl album. That created a new sound, known as scratching. Hip-hop's first MCs used the microphone simply to call out information, such as the time and date of the next party. Soon MCs turned these announcements into rhymes. Rap emerged when MCs put spoken-word lyrics over a DJ's thumping, rhythmic beat. Hip-hop's

B-girls and b-boys helped make break dancing one of hip-hop culture's signatures.

earliest lyrics, now referred to as old school style, had short lines, simple words, and easy rhymes. Rappers voiced creativity, joy, and energy.

First Female Hip-Hop Artists

Women contributed their talents to the four hip-hop art forms from the very beginning. When Kool Herc collected a group of MCs he called Herculords, he did not hesitate to ask girls, such as Pebblee Poo, to work the mic. MC Lisa Lee rocked the mic for DJ Afrika Bambaataa when she was 13.

Lady Pink (Sandra Fabara) was born in Ecuador but raised in Queens, New York City. She started tagging trains with her art and graffiti signature at age 15. From 1979 until 1985, she was one of the few, if not only, female artists working in the graffiti subculture. She was the only female member of graffiti crews TC5 (The Cool 5ive)

A POP STAR FAN OF RAP

Deborah Harry was the lead singer of Blondie, a pop group with an edgy, punk-rock sound. Harry saw Grandmaster Flash perform at a club. In Blondie's hit song "Rapture," not only did Harry rap, but she also added lyrics about the DJ: "Flash is fast, Flash is cool." The video played on Music Television (MTV) for several months, placing Grandmaster Flash in popular culture. "Rapture" opened the doors for other rock and pop groups to incorporate elements of hip-hop as well.

and TPA (The Public Animals). In a statement, she wrote, "The more guys said 'you can't do that', the more I had to prove them wrong."[2] As early as 1980, she gained recognition when her canvases were displayed in a New York art show. She started her own company in New York City to offer art workshops to kids, teenagers, and college students. Her canvases are in collections in the Whitney Museum, New York City's Met, the Brooklyn Museum, and even the Groninger Museum in Holland.

More women joined the scene. In 1993, Miss Van, originally from France, started painting *poupées,* which are cartoonish, doll-like women. For her depictions of the female form, she is known for starting a feminine movement in street art. In 2006, after studying art, Japanese-born Lady Aiko (born Aiko Nakagawa) started

TAGGING TRAINS

Graffiti emerged in New York City at the same time as hip-hop culture, and for the same reason—to rebel. Using spray paint, artists, who were mostly teenagers, "bombed" trains, turning cars into canvases and the subway system into moving art exhibits. Artists tagged, or signed, their murals in big or small letters, using aliases. Graffiti artists wanted to claim public space and fame. Some viewers, however, called graffiti vandalism. City officials treated it as a crime. Public perceptions changed somewhat when art collectors began buying graffiti canvases for high prices. In 2008, Lady Aiko and Lady Pink held a two-person show called "Brick Ladies" at a gallery in Brooklyn, New York City.

Lady Pink stands next to her artwork at the Graffiti Block Party in Chelsea, New York City, in 2005.

painting flowers in pink and purple colors and promoting a theme of love. She also uses stencils so that one image can appear in many public places. Maya Hayuk only works with art galleries who exhibit other women artists. Some women deliberately represent a female perspective.

Hip-Hop's Female Luminary Icon

Sha Rock (Sharon Green), born in 1962, was one of hip-hop's first MCs. She was approximately 12 years

old when she started break dancing as a b-girl. As early as 1976, when hip-hop was still local to the Bronx and before radio shows played rap, she wrote her own lyrics. As a performer, she loved the way MCs connected with audiences. As a resident of the South Bronx, she valued hip-hop's mission to foster communities in neighborhoods riddled with crime, drugs, and poverty. Sha Rock embraced hip-hop's principles of peace, unity, love, and fun.

Sha Rock was an original member of the group Funky 4+1. Working with Enjoy Records, Funky 4+1 signed one of hip-hop's first record deals. On the group's 1979 single "Rappin and Rocking the House," Sha Rock's lyrics introduced them: "They're four fly guys and the best female / I'm telling the truth, not a fairy tale." For her achievements and her influence on the evolution of the genre, she earned her titles Mother of the Mic and hip-hop's Luminary Icon. She went on to choose a career in law enforcement. In 2013, to promote hip-hop principles and educate young people about hip-hop culture, she founded Tomorrow's Footprints. This educational organization promotes fitness and dance.

The Mother of Hip-Hop

One woman saw the commercial potential of rap. She worked not as a performer but as a producer. Sylvia Robinson, an R&B singer and independent record producer, had a keen understanding of the music industry. Back in 1956, she released her own hit song "Love is

Strange." In the early 1960s, she and her husband, Joe, started operating All Platinum Records, an R&B label in Englewood, New Jersey. The small label was big enough to produce for musicians such as Ike & Tina Turner, and in 1973, Robinson recorded another hit of her own, "Pillow Talk." Still, those successes did not keep her business afloat.

By 1979, All Platinum went bankrupt. Robinson needed a new direction. She found it one June night at a niece's birthday party at Harlem World, a Manhattan nightclub, where she first heard rap. MC Lovebug Starski, who would soon write and produce with Salt-N-Pepa, one of the biggest female rap groups of all time, performed onstage. "A hip, hop/A hibbit a hop," he rapped to the beat. Robinson instantly recognized the electrifying impact of the spoken-word art form.

FUNKY 4+1 ON *SNL*

In 1981, on the recommendation of pop star Deborah Harry of Blondie, the group Funky 4+1 was invited to perform on the show *Saturday Night Live*. It was the first time rap musicians would appear on television. The show's producers, who hardly knew what rap music was, were nervous. Blondie's guitarist had to explain scratching to them. But the performance of "That's the Joint" was a success. Sha Rock, dressed simply in jeans, white boots, and a pink blouse, rapped old school lyrics: "Well, we just can't miss / with a beat like this." Funky 4+1 made history.

Rap's First Production Company

Robinson wanted to record a rap song. She set out to assemble a group of musicians on her own. She asked Lovebug Starski to be her MC, but he turned down the project. So, over the next few weeks, Robinson drove around New Jersey in search of MC talents. Three guys, Hank Jackson, Guy O'Brien, and Mike Wright, auditioned for her in the back of her car. Hank, on a break from his job at a pizza parlor, rapped for her while wearing his work apron. Robinson enlisted the three, called them the Sugarhill Gang, and renamed her record label Sugar Hill Records. In August 1979, over the melody and beat of a song called "Good Times," the MCs recorded "Rapper's Delight." The record was 15 minutes long.

> "Well I had never even heard anyone rap before, I just thought it was fabulous and I knew that minute that I had to put this new music onto a record."[4]
>
> —Sylvia Robinson, Dazed magazine, February 2000

DJs played it in clubs and on the radio. Club-goers, used to seeing MCs perform, heard recorded rap for the first time. Record stores sold out of the record as soon as they stocked more copies. When sales estimates reached two million, Billboard declared "Rapper's Delight" the

Robinson proved to be a highly successful businesswoman.

THE FIRST CREW: MERCEDES LADIES

Many young teenagers formed hip-hop groups—in the halls of high schools or in their neighborhoods. Founded in 1976, the Mercedes Ladies is considered the first all-female DJ and MC crew. With a core of six and then eight members, the group performed in parks and schools, often with others, such as Grandmaster Flash. Crew members purchased and carried their own turntables and crates of record albums. Other girls represented the Mercedes Ladies, wearing crew jackets to spread the name. "There was no money involved," said Sheri Sher, one of the group's first members. "It was for the street rep."[6] As big as hip-hop culture grew, it was heavily predicted to be nothing but a passing fad.

biggest seller ever made.[5] Sugar Hill Records became rap's first production company. This made Robinson hip-hop's first female producer. Under her label, Grandmaster Flash and the Furious Five recorded "Freedom" in 1980, the group's first song to hit the radio, and "The Message," which contained socially conscious lyrics. As one of the music industry's first producers, Robinson became known as the Mother of Hip-Hop.

Rap on the Radio

As more people embraced the hip-hop culture and craved the music, hip-hop expanded to areas outside of New York City. Philadelphia, Pennsylvania, native Lady B (Wendy Clark) had already recorded her own rap song, "To the Beat Y'All." The cut appeared on a Sugar

As of 2017, radio DJ Lady B was still broadcasting via Sirius XM Satellite Radio.

Hill compilation album. She was offered a job in radio in Philadelphia in 1979. As a radio DJ, she spun some of the hottest rap recordings. Ratings soared. From 1984 until 1989, Lady B ran the hit radio show "Street Beat," introducing new artists such as Public Enemy, Queen Latifah, Untouchable Force Organization (UTFO), MC Lyte, Run-D.M.C., LL Cool J, Big Daddy Kane, Rakim, KRS-One, Heavy D, and more. *Vibe* magazine has defined her as hip-hop's most influential female radio personality.[7] With rap music over the airwaves, hip-hop culture spread.

3 STANDING OUT

As hip-hop evolved and spread, it entered a golden era that lasted from approximately 1986 to 1994. Creative wordplay led to new lyric styles. Rhymes appeared internally, within the lines, not just at the end, and used multisyllabic words. MCs revealed a keen societal awareness, telling dark truths about inner-city life. Socially conscious rap lyrics protested poverty, violence, racism, and class struggles. Artists sampled more widely from soul, funk, jazz, and rock genres. During this era, artists such as Queen Latifah, MC Lyte, and Salt-N-Pepa had prolific creative output, along with fellow rappers such as LL Cool J, Ice-T, Public Enemy, and Run-D.M.C.

Salt-N-Pepa was one of the first mainstream all-female hip-hop groups.

Rap became a form of cultural communication. As rappers talked to each other through lyrics, rap grew confrontational. MCs bragged about their looks and rapping skills. They boasted about who was the best rapper. This led to competition and conflicts, either real or purely for show. MCs held verbal battles, or onstage contests in which they took turns insulting and taunting each other in rap form. They wrote and recorded songs, called diss songs, specifically intended to disrespect someone. Not all women engaged in battling. When Sha Rock performed with fellow MC Lisa Lee, everyone anticipated a battle-style rivalry. Instead, they formed a comradery, tossing the mic back and forth to take turns rapping.

Sha Rock, *left*, and Lisa Lee, *right*, appeared together with Debbie D, *center*, in the 1984 hip-hop movie *Beat Street*.

However, some songs demanded a response. In 1984, UTFO released "Roxanne, Roxanne." In the song, three bragging male MCs describe being turned down by the same girl: "She was walking down the street so I said 'Hello / I'm Kangol from UTFO.' And she said 'So?'" By future standards, the rhymes were gentle and funny. Still, the hit radio song seemed to disrespect the fictional Roxanne. Someone had to represent her in a counter song. One MC accepted the challenge.

The Diss: The Roxanne Wars

Born on November 9, 1969, Lolita Shanté Gooden grew up in Queensbridge public housing. Located in Long Island City, part of Queens borough, across from Manhattan on the other side of the Queensboro Bridge, it is the largest housing project in North America and the home and birthplace of Nas and other future rappers. By 1980, at age 11, Lolita was rhyming. She was only 14 when, using the name Roxanne Shanté, she answered UTFO's song with "Roxanne's Revenge," hip-hop's first recorded diss song.

Speaking as the girl in UTFO's song, she claimed to tell the real story about three guys who failed to win her attention. She freestyled instead of writing lyrics down.

Roxanne Shanté's "Roxanne's Revenge" defined her as a battle MC.

LATIN QUARTER NIGHTCLUB

In the early 1980s, Latin Quarter was a hot rap club at the corner of Forty-Eighth Street and Broadway in Manhattan. It was one of the few musical places in Times Square that allowed people in under the age of 21. There, rap groups such as Public Enemy, Run-D.M.C., and the Jungle Brothers took the stage. Stars who would later perform, such as Queen Latifah and Lil' Kim, were teenagers in the audience.

In 1984, her response song made a huge splash. She was prompted to perform more diss songs. She competed in Manhattan nightclubs, such as Latin Quarter, and toured to other cities. Two years later, at age 16 and pregnant with her first child, her priorities changed, and she withdrew from hip-hop. She retired from hip-hop at age 25. The success of "Roxanne's Revenge," however, lured others into the recording business.

Let's Talk About It: Salt-N-Pepa

Soon, another diss song led to the creation of what would become one of rap's most popular female duos and then trio: Salt-N-Pepa. Deidra Roper joined later, but in 1985, Salt (Cheryl James) and Pepa (Sandy Denton), both from Queens, were studying to be nurses when fellow classmate Lovebug Starski asked them to help him record a diss song for a class project. Salt-N-Pepa's answer to a popular song called "The Show" by Doug E. Fresh was

Salt-N-Pepa members pose with their awards after the 37th Annual Grammy Awards in 1995.

"The Showstopper." But Salt-N-Pepa didn't want to write diss songs. They wanted to talk to women about women's issues. The next singles made a bigger impact. The group's 1987 song "Tramp" was promoted to be a single. However, on the other side of the record, called the B-side, was another song that was much more popular with fans. "Push It" went mainstream and earned a Grammy nomination. "Push It" was released when talking about sex was taboo. The simple lyrics are not overtly sexual: "Ooh baby, baby," and "Push it, push it real good." But it was clear Salt-N-Pepa was advocating for a woman's enjoyment of her physical body, whether through dancing uninhibitedly or expressing sexual desires.

Wearing trendy clothes—jackets with shoulder pads, acid-wash jeans, and midriff tops—Salt-N-Pepa urged women to have self-respect and end abusive relationships. They criticized society for shaming women's behaviors. Their 1991 song "Let's Talk About Sex," from *Blacks' Magic*, which features Dee Dee Roper, known as DJ Spinderella, topped US and international charts. Later, they tweaked the song for an awareness campaign, writing "Let's Talk About AIDS." It was Salt-N-Pepa's next album, *Very Necessary*, released in 1993, that made it the best-selling female rap group. The album sold five million copies and contains the hit "None of Your Business."[1] For the song, Salt-N-Pepa won Best Rap Performance by a

> "[Salt-N-Pepa] behaved like they were as empowered as the male rappers. The theme of female empowerment thumps through almost every track on every album."[2]
>
> —Sarah Oakes, "Why Salt-N-Pepa were 20 Years Ahead of their Time," DailyLife.com, April 6, 2015

Duo or Group at the 1995
Grammy Awards.

MCs in the House

Queen Latifah (Dana Owens)
was in the audience at
Latin Quarter the first time
Salt-N-Pepa performed.
She also saw DJ Jazzy Joyce
and MC Sweet Tee who, she
recalled, "ripped the mike
with her vocals."[3] These role
models gave her the courage
to get up onstage herself.
Her fellow MCs called her
Princess of the Posse. The
royalty theme gave Queen
Latifah confidence. She took
the stage wearing hats and
jackets sewn from African
fabrics. Sometimes she wore
a crown. Rapping freestyle,
she borrowed reggae sounds
and African words. She called
for respect for women and

QUEEN LATIFAH

In 1988, Queen Latifah released
a single, "Wrath of My Madness,"
with "Princess of the Posse"
on the B-side. After Queen
Latifah signed a record deal with
Tommy Boy Entertainment, her
first album, *All Hail the Queen*,
was released in 1989. She
was 19 years old. She rapped
about self-respect while the
group 45 King provided the
beats. *All Hail the Queen* was
one of the best-selling rap
albums of the decade. In 1995,
Queen Latifah won the Best
Rap Solo Performance Grammy
for her hit single "U.N.I.T.Y." At
the Soul Train Music Awards,
she won the Sammy Davis Jr.
Award for Entertainer of the
Year. She founded Flavor Unit
Entertainment. She still serves
as CEO for the record company.
Queen Latifah published her
memoir, *Ladies First*, in 1999.
In 2004, she sang jazz vocals
for her album *The Dana Owens
Album*. She has gone on to a
successful acting career, earning
an Academy Award nomination
for her role as prison warden
in *Chicago*.

all people and spoke out against violence.

At the time, few rappers came from New Jersey. She changed that by calling out, "New Jersey's in the house!" She did not rap about topics such as losing or needing a man, which were considered a woman's domain. Instead, when she launched her debut album *All Hail the Queen*, she challenged stereotypes. "I'm living positive, not out here knocked up," she raps on her song "Evil That Men Do." By presenting herself as a strong, independent woman, Queen Latifah provided an alternative role model and broke hip-hop barriers for women.

Latifah would become good friends with MC Lyte (Lana Moorer). Lyte started rapping at age 12 and had a single at age 16. In 1988, *Lyte as a Rock* was the first album ever recorded by a solo female rapper. MC Lyte realized she could add something new to all the boasting and dissing. She used rap to tell narrative stories. In her first rap, "I Cram to Understand U (Sam)," a jealous narrator believes her boyfriend is cheating on her. He is, but her rival isn't another girl; it is his addiction to drugs.

When Lyte toured, she often found herself sharing the stage with an all-male lineup of stars, such as Heavy D, Fresh Prince (Will Smith), and MC Hammer. She had to advocate for herself to maintain her place with them, both on and off the stage. In the next phase of hip-hop, the rise of gangsta rap would continue to challenge female rappers. Some proved to be as tough as their male counterparts, while others provided a point of view that set them apart from the men.

MC LYTE SUPPORTS FELLOW FEMALES

To promote rap and hip-hop artists, MC Lyte joined the Governor's Board of the Recording Academy's Los Angeles chapter in 2011. She became the chapter's first African-American female president. "I got involved to help shape the future of the music I loved," she wrote.[5] MC Lyte also started a foundation called Hip Hop Sisters. The foundation offers hip-hop scholarships, mentoring, and retreats while it promotes positive images for women and men.

BEHIND
THE SONG

QUEEN LATIFAH'S "LADIES FIRST"

In the 1980s, artists made music videos to accompany their songs. At the time, it was rare for a woman to write and record her own songs. In "Ladies First," a song from Queen Latifah's album *All Hail the Queen*, Queen Latifah maintains creative control and stands up for herself and all women. The music video is critical of sexism and racism. Queen Latifah flashes pictures of African-American leaders, such as abolitionist Harriet Tubman, former slave Sojourner Truth, and political activist Angela Davis. She raps: "Now, it's time to rhyme. Can you relate to a sister dope enough to make you holler and scream?" Throughout the video, she adds historic context with footage of war, protests, and civil rights activism.

Queen Latifah also presented a strong image of herself in the video. Styling herself as a military leader in a suit of African colors, she embraces her African-American culture while criticizing the racism of South Africa. Her lyrics promote women's importance, demand equality, and encourage women to support one another. Her song, which featured a British MC, Monie Love, is considered a historic piece.

Queen Latifah often dressed in African-inspired clothing, as seen here in her 1989 MTV Video Music Awards appearance.

4 CHANGING IMAGES FOR WOMEN

With the birth of hip-hop, an entire culture of people had a powerful vehicle of expression. Increasingly, rappers used it to voice rage and rebellion against violence, poverty, apathy, and unrest. MCs rapped about social injustice, power, race, and sexuality. As the 1980s ended, an era of innocence in rap also seemed to end as gangsta rap emerged. MC Lyte and Queen Latifah had created modest rap personas compared to the bold sexuality that appeared in the 1990s. In 1996, during a peak year for rap, artists such as Lil' Kim, with her debut album *Hard Core*, and Foxy Brown, with her debut album *Ill Na Na*, represented a female point of view that was described as vulgar and raw. These female rappers were the new thing.

Lil' Kim chose to wear more-revealing clothing to portray her tough and sexy attitude.

J. J. Fad's Commercial Success

One all-female West Coast group came on the scene just before gangsta rap. J. J. Fad represented the tail end of the 1980s. Its name stood for Just Jammin', Fresh and Def, and the group members were MCs J.B. (Juana Burns), Baby-D (Dania Birks), and Sassy C (Michelle Franklin). In 1988, they created a catchy dance song titled "Supersonic." The hit stayed on *Billboard* charts for eight weeks. J. J. Fad became the first all-female rap posse to earn a Grammy nomination for Best Rap Performance. To match their fun lyrics, members of J. J. Fad wore oversized letter jackets with spandex pants. They accessorized with heavy gold chains, running shoes, and Rollerblades. J. J. Fad achieved commercial success. Eazy-E, Dr. Dre, and Ice Cube, as N.W.A, dropped *Straight Outta Compton* and changed the face of rap.

Donning a different look from their earlier days, members of J. J. Fad performed together at Back to the Eighties in New York City in 2012.

Gangsta Rap

Gangsta rap erupted from the realities of life in South Central Los Angeles neighborhoods, such as Compton. With *Straight Outta Compton*, N.W.A led the way. In a tone of rage, the group protested injustice, racism, police brutality, and violence. In 1992, N.W.A split up. The members went on to do their own projects. Dr. Dre made *The Chronic* and launched the career of Snoop Dogg, who made the hit album *Doggystyle*. But N.W.A's explosive album helped define the 1990s. A gangsta rap rivalry started between East Coast and West Coast rappers, highlighted mainly by the Notorious B.I.G., who represented the East Coast, and Tupac Shakur, who represented the West Coast. In the face of this new aggression, women of rap quickly grew emboldened. The 1980s trends, such as that of J. J. Fad, were about to give way to something entirely new.

Yo-Yo Represents the West Coast

Yo-Yo, born Yolanda Whitaker Winsome in 1971, was familiar with gang violence, having grown up in South Central Los Angeles. As a kid, Roxanne Shanté inspired her. But it was Ice Cube who provoked her to rhyme harder. When they battled in his song "It's a Man's World," she rhymed just as tough as him, challenging his demeaning lyrics. "Stay down and play the playground you little girl," Ice Cube taunted. Yo-Yo responded with lines such as, "Well I'm not your puppet so don't even try to pull." When he rapped, "Women, they're good for nothing," she responded with, "Downing a girl, first offense, and that's a no-no." The song appeared on Ice Cube's debut solo album, *AmeriKKKa's Most Wanted*, in 1990. That same

Yo-Yo performs at friend Queen Latifah's birthday party in 2009.

year, at the age of 18, Yo-Yo released her own single, "You Can't Play With My Yo-Yo." Her lyrics state her purpose, to uplift women. Many fans recognized her work as an attack against misogyny, contempt toward women, and sexism in rap music. In 1991, Yo-Yo's debut album, *Make Way for the Motherlode*, introduced the IBWC, Intelligent Black Women's Coalition, a support group she formed to promote self-esteem for women. Yo-Yo and Ice Cube remained strong working partners, and many of Yo-Yo's songs feature Ice Cube.

Being part of the era gave Yo-Yo a voice. "I knew instinctively that hip-hop could be a means of communication and empowerment," she said.[2] However, when the trend for women turned sexy, she felt she had no place. "If that was the direction music was going," Yo-Yo said, "I wasn't going to be able to

DA BRAT'S HARD STYLE

Born in 1974 and raised in Chicago, Illinois, Da Brat (Shawntae Harris) had the hard style that typified the 1990s, but she did not embrace the sexy image of some of her contemporaries. She dressed in baggy jeans and jerseys. After releasing another popular album, *Anuthatantrum*, in 1996, she made cameo appearances on the albums of Missy Elliott, Lil' Kim, Mariah Carey, and others. For her 2000 album, *Unrestricted*, she cultivated a sexier look. A *Rolling Stone* review noted she sounded sultry without acting like a sex kitten.[3]

participate."[4] Yo-Yo went to college, studying business and acting. She returned to rap long enough to drop her last albums, *Total Control* in 1996 and *Ebony* in 1998.

Rap Turns Sexy

Only a few years after J. J. Fad and Salt-N-Pepa wore zippered athletic jackets and spandex pants, rap fashions changed. With gangsta rap, women's fashions increasingly moved from tough to sexy. As the production quality of song videos improved, music's visual element put more emphasis on fashion trends and appearances. Though gangsta rap started in order to protest violence, during the 1990s, it seemed to reach fantasy levels. Some songs focused more on entertainment value than a social message. In their videos, male rappers characterized themselves as pimps, mobsters, and crime lords gripping wads of cash, surrounded by luxury cars, jewelry, and women. In response to this male posturing, women rappers provided some posturing of their own.

> "Women have always been a presence in male-founded hip-hop groups. . . . The woman is either the hypersexualized mascot or the secret-weapon anomaly that proves—surprise!—girls can rap, too."[5]
>
> —*Janelle Harris*, Atlantic *magazine, 2016*

LIL' KIM

Born in 1975, in Brooklyn, Lil' Kim (Kimberly Denise Jones) had a childhood marked by abuse, homelessness, and rebellion. In her friendship with Notorious B.I.G. (Christopher Wallace), she found a mentor. In 1995, she joined his group Junior M.A.F.I.A.—Masters At Finding Intelligent Attitudes. On the album *Conspiracy*, she made "Player's Anthem" and "Get Money" hit songs. Notorious B.I.G. called her "the dopest female MC that's coming out ever."[7] Her later albums, *The Notorious K.I.M.* in 2000, and *La Bella Mafia* in 2003, were certified platinum.

The 1990s was a decade of materialism, and everything was for sale, including sex. Women found ways to respond to male videos. Against male imagery, wearing leopard-print lingerie under a luxurious mink coat, for example, or other vivid clothing, MC Lil' Kim projected a tough and sexy attitude. At first, even her record company didn't understand the new look. "They thought I needed to . . . wear sweat suits and all that," said Kim.[6] Her solo album, *Hard Core*, arrived in the middle of the gangsta era, in 1996. It went double platinum with number one hits "No Time," "Not Tonight," and "Crush on You." Some people credit *Hard Core* with starting new X-rated trends.

At the same time as Lil' Kim's *Hard Core*, in 1996, Foxy Brown dropped her debut album. Brown, who was raised in Brooklyn, was 17 when she released her landmark album *Ill Na Na.* Blatant, forceful, and commanding lyrics defined Foxy as a so-called bad girl in control, a mirror to the bad boy image of male rappers.

Eve joined Foxy Brown and Lil' Kim at the top of the charts. She started rapping when she was 12. She dyed her hair blond and, later, bright red. At 18, she got her signature tattoo—paw prints on her chest—which further defined her as a tough and sexy woman on the hip-hop scene. When Eve was 19, a record deal with Dr. Dre in Los Angeles confirmed rap was her life's mission. Back in Philadelphia, she became the first woman to sign with the record label Ruff Ryders Entertainment. In 1999, she dropped her debut album, *Let There Be Eve…Ruff Ryders' First Lady.* Eve became the third female MC, after Lauryn Hill and Foxy Brown, with a number one album. Hers sold 213,000 copies in the first week.[8] Provocative images of women were

THE COLOR PLATINUM

The Recording Industry Association of America (RIAA) awards big-selling albums. Albums are gold if they sell 500,000 copies. When sales reach one million copies, albums are certified platinum. The first platinum album by a female rap act was Salt-N-Pepa's 1986 album *Hot, Cool & Vicious.* The first female solo rap album to go platinum was *Funkdafied* by Da Brat in 1994. Other artists who've gone platinum since are Lil' Kim, Foxy Brown, Eve, Lauryn Hill, Missy Elliott, and Nicki Minaj.

EVE LOOKS BACK

On his show, Larry King introduced Eve as a "rapper, actor, and pit bull in a skirt." It was a name she'd called herself, back when the Ruff Ryders called themselves dogs. He cited French Montana's quote, "Female rappers have to be bulletproof." Eve did not disagree. "You have to be one of the boys," she said, "but still be able to be a female."[9] She presented a tough attitude. Today, she says that when people meet her, they are surprised she is so nice.

controversial, but they also started a conversation about double standards. If male rappers could brag about their sex appeal, Foxy Brown and Lil' Kim suggested women should be able to do the same.

With artists such as Lauryn Hill, Missy Elliott, Lil' Kim, Foxy Brown, and Eve all on the scene at the same time, it was clear women in the industry had choices. Women in rap had also reached the point where they could decide whether to be in charge of their own music.

Eve at the 2000 American Music Awards, wearing the Ruff Ryder emblem

5 WOMEN IN CHARGE

In 1995, it was a woman's idea to blend hip-hop and R&B. Producer Sylvia Rhone invited rappers Queen Latifah, MC Lyte, and Yo-Yo to join R&B singer Brandy in a 1995 remix of her single, "I Wanna Be Down." Rhone is considered one of the biggest executives in music. The remix not only added rap to the song, but it seemed to demonstrate women helping each other.

Missy Elliott is another female artist who recognized production as a way to control her own work. She took charge of her own career from the beginning. In 1996, she launched her career as a guest rapper on other artists' songs. When she rapped on Gina Thompson's remix "The Things That You Do," Sean "Puff Daddy"

Missy Elliott is known for her creative production work in addition to her own rapping skills.

TOP MUSIC EXECUTIVE

Sylvia Rhone is a major figure in the music industry. In 1990, when she was hired as CEO and president of Atlantic's East/West Records, she became the first African-American woman to head a major record company. In 1994, she went on to be chairman and CEO of Elektra, this time being the first African American to hold the title. As president of Universal Motown Records from 2004 until 2011, Rhone oversaw artists such as Lil Wayne, Nicki Minaj, Drake, Kid Cudi, Nelly, and Erykah Badu. In 2012, she became CEO of her own label, Vested in Culture.

Combs produced it with his company Bad Boy Records. Elliott also guest rapped in MC Lyte's single "Cold Rock a Party" in 1996.

In those two cases, Missy was a performer. At the same time, she knew producers had more control than musicians. She created her own production team, working with Timbaland (Timothy Mosely), her longtime friend and creative partner. For singer Aaliyah Dana Houghton, they wrote and produced seven songs on her 1996 album, *One in a Million*. The multitalented Elliott added background vocals to nearly every track. In the video for the hit single "If Your Girl Only Knew," several stars made cameos—Elliott, Timbaland, 702, Lil' Kim, Ginuwine, and Aaliyah's brother Rashad. *One in a Million* went double platinum. With that success, Elliott and Timbaland shot to stardom. They produced other artists, such as Destiny's Child. Elliott was involved in every part of hip-hop's network.

Part of Elliott's success is her love of collaborating with other artists. In 1997, Elliott was featured in Lil' Kim's remix of "Not Tonight," along with Angie Martinez, Da Brat, and Lisa "Left Eye" Lopes. To remix her own song, "Sock it 2 Me," Elliott asked Da Brat to deliver her rapid rap lyrics. In 2000, Elliott produced a remake of a popular 1975 disco song, "Lady Marmalade." She brought in pop singers Christina Aguilera, Pink, and Mya. The addition of Lil' Kim added hip-hop to its French cabaret style. The song blew up the pop charts.

> "If you ran into Missy, you would say, 'This is a ghetto girl with ghetto curls.' Underneath the 'hee-hee haw-haw,' she's one of the sharpest businesswomen I've ever come up against."[1]
>
> — *Sylvia Rhone*, The New Yorker, *1997*

Rap as Performance

Since the 1980s, when making a music video became a required part of promoting a new song, it became increasingly important for musicians to craft both their musical abilities and their public image. Missy Elliott did not conform to conventional standards of beauty. She is a performance artist. She dressed in blown-up garbage

From left to right, Lil' Kim, Pink, Mya, and Christina Aguilera perform "Lady Marmalade" at the 2001 MTV Movie Awards, for which they won a Grammy.

bags and inflatable body suits for her groundbreaking video of "The Rain (Supa Dupa Fly)." For her video "I'm Really Hot," she wore parachute pants and a puffy jacket. When she donned costumes rather than designer clothes,

she showed both a keen attention to style and a sense of humor. She chose to present herself as neither hard nor sexy. Instead of following trends, she invented her own unique creations.

FORMING A PARTNERSHIP

Introduced by friends, Missy Elliott met Timbaland (Tim Mosely) in the late 1980s, when they were both in high school. He had built a small studio in his house in Portsmouth, Virginia. She went there one day and listened to his tapes. Elliott and Timbaland connected instantly. She liked his unique sound. What he noticed most about her, besides her talent, was her determination. After that meeting, they worked together almost every day.

Elliott's song "4 My People" features Eve on the album *Miss E . . . So Addictive*. Using explicit lyrics and profanity, the two MCs describe partying with drugs and alcohol and desiring sex. "The music's bangin, way down in my soul / When you dance behind me, I lose all control," Elliott raps. When she buys drinks, she says, "I got this feeling, and it's all over me." When she is attracted to someone, she wants to "lick your face." And on the dance floor, she wants "to feel some ecstasy." These themes are not atypical of rap music. However, Elliott and Eve successfully used sexuality and rough language in a way that their female fans could relate to, in a way that did not seem offensive or gratuitous. Perhaps it is because the MCs describe only their own experiences. The lyrics do not confront, challenge, or insult anyone else. In a bar, the same kind of setting where violence can happen, they

Elliott broke style constructs of the time by performing in creative costumes, such as blown-up garbage bags.

express a sense of joy and fun. The song is about the pleasure of being alive.

People who know Elliott recognize her smart, savvy business sense. She succeeded by making smart decisions in the industry and by maintaining control of her own creative decisions. And while some performers spent excessively, she saved and invested her earnings. She

COMMUNITY COLLABORATION

Musicians rarely work alone. John Legend was a little-known college student when he played piano on Lauryn Hill's song "Everything is Everything." The legendary Carlos Santana added his signature guitar styling to Hill's song "To Zion." She provided lead vocals for "Do You Like the Way," a track on his album *Supernatural*. By the end of the 1990s, it seemed like everyone knew each other. Musicians formed alliances with each other, both within and outside of the rap genre. They produced for each other, wrote songs for each other, and appeared on each other's records.

achieved fame and success by working on both sides of the music business. She is a songwriter, video director, and record label owner. She is both an artist and a producer. Women such as Missy Elliott and Sylvia Rhone set new industry standards. However, even as rap music continued to grow, so did controversy around the ways women were represented in rap music.

Elliott sings into her Grammy, awarded for Best Female Rap Solo Performance, at the 46th Annual Grammy Awards in 2004.

6 RAP, POP, AND
WOMEN

In 2003, many listeners got a surprise when they heard a rap song on popular music radio stations. "Where Is the Love?" by the Black Eyed Peas contained enough pop elements to earn broader radio play. With a melodic chorus written by pop star Justin Timberlake, the socially conscious message expressed a heartfelt plea for peace following the terrorist attacks on New York City on September 11, 2001. The group's original members, Taboo, Apl.de.ap, and will.i.am, had already put out two albums. The song appeared on their third effort, *Elephunk*, their first album to include Fergie (Stacy Ferguson). Fergie added strong vocals and a feminine presence, as well as a unifying element.

Fergie performs "Where Is the Love?" as a member of the Black Eyed Peas at the 46th Annual Grammy Awards.

While other rap songs portrayed a degrading image of women, "Where Is the Love?" was an anomaly. With long, blonde hair, dressed in khakis and a tank top, Fergie faced the camera and the microphone as an equal member of the group. One critic wrote that the song provided an alternative to "all the macho posturing in rap and the shallowness of pop."[1] Whenever rap music entered the arena of popular music, it gained more media attention. And as rap earned that attention, the media helped shape the nation's understanding of the rap community. As a conversation about rap in general grew, public conversation about rap's relationship to women also grew.

Addressing the Representation of Women in Rap

As male rappers continued to depict women as objects of domination and violence, society began to grapple with difficult questions. Can rap videos be blamed for sexism?

Fergie has gone on to create solo tracks, always with her own confident sense of style.

HISTORY OF RAP IN POP MUSIC

As early as 1980, hip-hop surfaced in mainstream culture. In the 1983 movie *Flashdance*, a dancer impresses judges by break dancing during an audition. In 1984, R&B singer Chaka Khan recorded a remake of a Prince song—"I Feel for You." Her version was full of hip-hop influences. It was filmed on a stage designed with graffiti art. Break dancers performed in the background, and MC Melle Mel rapped an introduction to the song. Gradually, barriers broke down between rap and pop.

In July 1990, the pop song "She Ain't Worth It" by Glenn Madeiros featured rapper Bobby Brown. It opened the door for rappers to collaborate on pop songs. Janet Jackson's "Got Til It's Gone," in 1997, featured rapper Q-Tip and sampled from "Big Yellow Taxi," a 1970 song by folk singer Joni Mitchell. Jennifer Lopez's "I'm Real (Remix)" featured Ja Rule in 2001. That same year, two of Eve's songs, "Who's That Girl" and "Let Me Blow Ya Mind," both featured pop singer Gwen Stefani. Beyoncé's "Crazy in Love," in 2003, featured Jay Z. Pop and rap artistic collaborations dissolved borders between genres. The songs allowed musicians increased freedom to use elements of rap.

Eve and Gwen Stefani's "Let Me Blow Ya Mind" earned a Grammy in 2002 for Best Rap/Sung Collaboration.

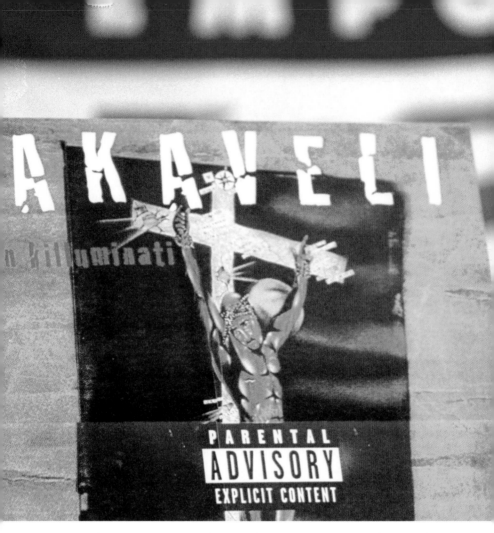

Politician C. DeLores Tucker waged a campaign against profanity and violence in music, using a Tupac Shakur album as an example.

Does rap music actually promote violence against women? These questions opened an ongoing public conversation. In 2005, to address those issues, the Center for the Study of Race, Politics, and Culture at the University of Chicago held a conference on hip-hop and feminism. It was the first of its kind. Scholars, students, artists, activists,

and community members discussed the relationship
between rap music and violence against women.

Attendees watched *Hip-Hop Gurlz*, an eight-minute
documentary made by then-22-year-old Tamika Guishard.
To explore the influence of rap music videos on the
self-esteem of young girls, she interviewed a *Vibe*

magazine editor, an MTV producer, and young hip-hop fans. "I do love hip-hop," she said. "Don't get it twisted. But it's just that sometimes I feel like hip-hop doesn't love me back."[2] She saw that hip-hop had reduced itself to containing three elements: a beat, lyrics, and objectified women. "What hip-hop fails to realize," said MTV News producer Morenike Efutande, "is that there are a lot of girls who are fans of hip-hop, and it puts them in a funny position because they're being objectified."[3]

Byron Hurt believes that to shed light on why women are objectified, it is important to examine hip-hop's definition of masculinity and manhood. He believes male stereotypes are in part responsible for the counterpart of female stereotypes. In his documentary *Hip-Hop Beyond Beats & Rhymes*, he explores misogyny, homophobia, and violence in rap. "America is a very hyper-masculinized, hyper-aggressive nation," Hurt asserts—not just in rap but in film and television, in sports, in military culture, and elsewhere.[4] Hurt's theory is that gangsta rap caricaturized black masculinity, creating an exaggerated, distorted stereotype of black men as thugs, pimps, and criminals. The images influenced men to act tough and uncaring, for example, or they would be ridiculed for being weak and bullied for showing emotions.

Violence in the Industry

The 2005 conference was a step in the right direction. Discussing the problems brought awareness to, but did not solve, issues of domestic violence. On February 8, 2009, during a heated argument, 19-year-old singer Chris Brown punched, bit, and choked artist Rihanna, his 20-year-old girlfriend. Brown was arrested and charged with two felonies. Rihanna was hospitalized. Publicly leaked photos of her bruised and swollen face drew a public outcry against domestic violence. A devastated hip-hop community responded with support for Rihanna.

Some theories suggest that children who grow up in abusive households

RIHANNA

Born in 1988 in Barbados, Rihanna (Robyn Rihanna Fenty) grew up influenced by pop, reggae, R&B, and rap. In 2005, at age 16, she landed a recording contract with Jay Z, president of Def Jam Records. Her debut album, *Music of the Sun*, dropped eight months later. Her steady release of new albums brought her to stardom. She has worked with some of rap's biggest male MCs. Her song "Umbrella" features Jay Z. His song "Run This Town" features both Rihanna and Kanye West. And Rihanna is featured on Kanye West's song "All of the Lights." She sings in Drake's songs "Take Care" and "What's My Name?" and is featured on Eminem's hit "Love the Way You Lie." She worked with Nicki Minaj on "Raining Men" and "Fly." Often, she sings the chorus, adding her melodic voice to the rap songs and helping rap songs achieve the same success as pop.

In addition to collaborating on tracks with other artists, Rihanna records and performs solo, often touring around the world.

are more likely to suffer or commit domestic violence. As a child, Rihanna witnessed her father beating her mother. Likewise, Brown's stepfather beat his mother. Three years later, to the confusion and dismay of her public supporters, Rihanna returned to her relationship with Brown.

In November 2006, Oprah Winfrey interviewed Sean Combs, asking him about rap's controversial treatment of women. She asked him if it was possible for rap lyrics to stop demeaning women. He said yes. "Demeaning women is not right," he said. "Violence is not right. Evil is not right." But, he added, hip-hop did not invent violence. Instead, it reflected it. Though he agreed with Oprah, saying, "Hip-hop still has a lot of evolving to do," he added that hip-hop has also "given our youth more joy and hope and a better form of release than almost anything out there."[5] The next generation of women in rap would speak out more frankly and personally against abuse and domestic violence.

"Because life is not perfect, and the minute you feel it's perfect, it's not real. Artists sign a deal to make music; we didn't sign to be perfect, or to be role models. We're all flawed human beings who are learning and growing and evolving."[6]

—Rihanna, Vanity Fair, 2015

7 MAINSTREAM AND INDIE STARS

The first two decades of the twenty-first century saw a rise of artists working in underground music, either to launch their careers to mainstream status or to have more freedom of artistic choice. By some definitions, underground artists are simply less popular. By others, underground artists are less commercial. Mainstream music sells, while underground music does not. Mainstream artists are in the spotlight, receiving more media attention. Underground artists have more control over their songs, signing with smaller independent labels. Some artists remain independent by choice. Others strive for the mainstream limelight.

Nicki Minaj is a leading female hip-hop icon.

MINAJ'S INFLUENCES AND IDOL

Minaj grew up with a diverse range of musical tastes. Her rap influences include Lisa "Left Eye" Lopes and TLC, Lauryn Hill, Remy Ma, Lil' Kim, and Missy Elliott. Outside of rap, she's a fan of Grace Jones and Cyndi Lauper. Minaj has her own idol—R&B singer Monica. To practice, Minaj used to sing like her, reaching the low notes and practicing riffs. While Minaj was on her *Pinkprint* tour in 2012, Monica even joined her onstage for Minaj's performance in Atlanta, Georgia.

New Millennium

Nicki Minaj (Onika Tanya Maraj) is considered one of rap's biggest female stars. She did not start out there. She was born in Trinidad in 1982 and raised in Queens. In high school, she studied theater at the Upper West Side's Fiorello H. Laguardia High School of Music & Art and Performing Arts, worked as a waitress, and practiced freestyling on her lunch breaks. In 2002, she was a member of the Hoodstars. When the rap group failed to get a recording contract, Minaj released her solo mixtapes *Playtime is Over* in 2007 and *Sucka Free* in 2008. She won Female Artist of the Year at the 2008 Underground Music Awards. With her distinct, melodic voice, she wouldn't stay in hip-hop's underground for long. Her third mixtape, *Beam Me Up Scotty*, released in 2009, won the attention of Lil Wayne, who helped her sign with his label, Young Money Entertainment.

Minaj is known for her outlandish costumes.

Minaj's theater background helped her become a performer. She grew up in an abusive family environment and prefers to keep aspects of her background private. Masking herself in elaborate costumes, Minaj almost hides behind her music personae. To portray Harajuku Barbie, she sings in a higher-pitched voice. In songs such as "Roman Holiday," she is Roman Zolanski, a paranoid and violent gay male alter ego. She plays Martha Zolanski, his mother, in "Roman's Revenge" and "Moment 4 Life." She also uses story elements. In "Your Love," Minaj uses a martial arts theme, posing as a karate student and then as a geisha in a kimono. In "Moment 4 Life," featuring Drake, Minaj borrows from the fairy tale Cinderella, dressing in ball gowns.

Indie Stars

Some artists start on smaller independent labels. If they get enough notice and popularity, they might sign with larger, more commercial labels. Sri Lankan British artist

M.I.A. gained worldwide recognition. In 2009, *Time* magazine placed her in the *Time* list of "The 100 Most Influential People."

Another artist, Angel Haze (born 1991) seemed poised to break into commercial recording. But after one album with a major label, the talented artist returned to working independently. With rap, Haze channeled rage over a childhood marked by trauma and sexual abuse. Working independently provided freedom to be honest about it. In 2006, at age 15, the Detroit, Michigan, native moved to New York City with her mother to escape their membership in a repressive religious organization. She began making tracks and was noticed for her rapid-fire lyrics. To deliver them, she trained her mouth to stay loose and her jaw not to lock up. Her song "Cleaning Out My Closet," from her 2012 mixtape *Classick*, is partly an homage to her idol Eminem, who has a song with the same title. It is mostly, however, a painfully brutal, rage-filled account of surviving the nightmare of sexual abuse.

"I never want to get too complacent with my writing or my flow. I love that people never know what Nicki they are going to get on a particular song. I like bringing out a different side. I think that's what rappers should do. I pride myself on always having a magical moment."[2]

—*Nicki Minaj*, Vogue, 2015

ANGEL HAZE

Angel Haze is mixed race and identifies as pansexual or agender. Family life in Detroit included membership in a strict religious group, the Pentecostal Greater Apostolic Faith. For three years, from age seven to ten, Haze was a victim of sexual abuse. From this abusive, repressive background, Haze went to New York City. At age 16, the first time the rapper heard Eminem, Haze found a fitting art form. Rap was the outlet that allowed Haze true expression.

Haze now identifies as agender and is a social activist for LGBTQ rights, fiercely protesting any form of abuse. After releasing mixtapes *New Moon*, *Altered Ego*, *King*, *Voice*, and *Reservation* for free on the Internet, Haze released *Dirty Gold* through Island Records in 2013. Soon after, Haze left the label. In 2015, the rapper self-released another free mixtape, *Back to the Woods*.

Some reviewers observed that working independently afforded Haze the opportunity for true artistic expression.

Similar to Haze, from a young age, Azealia Banks (born 1991) longed to be a performer, in part to escape an abusive home life. Raised in Harlem by a single mom, Banks attended Laguardia High School. At age ten, she acted off-Broadway with the Tada! Youth Theater. After starring in several productions, she considered breaking into television roles but chose rap instead. In 2008, at 16, she released "Seventeen." In 2011, struggling to pay rent, she released "212," a hot song with an irresistible dance beat. She spent 30 dollars on a low-budget but compelling black-and-white video for "212." In it, she wears a single outfit—cutoff shorts and a Mickey Mouse sweatshirt—rapping in front of a brick wall, sometimes

Angel Haze performs at the AfroPunk Fest in Brooklyn in August 2016.

Azealia Banks performs at Coachella in 2015.

up close. The song received rave reviews, and the video went viral. In 2012, Banks released a mixtape called *1991*. Three years later, after clashing with three major labels, she self-released her full-length debut, *Broke With Expensive Taste.*

Rap music had white male artists, such as the Beastie Boys, Eminem, and Macklemore, but not any white female artists. Australian artist Iggy Azalea moved to the United States in 2006, living in Miami, Houston, and Atlanta before going to Los Angeles in 2010. In that time, she developed a southern accent. Some critics call her style electro-rap. She actively sought a record deal from a major label. She released *The New Classic* through Def Jam in 2014. With her single "Fancy," she was the fourth solo female rapper to top the *Billboard* Hot 100. She earned four Grammy nominations. In 2014, her songs held the top two spots on the *Billboard* chart.[3]

SHA ROCK ON NEW RAP

In an interview, old school MC Sha Rock was pressed to speak about the commercial success of white rappers such as Iggy Azalea and Macklemore. "Rap music within the culture is not just for African Americans," Sha Rock said. "It's for anybody that decides that they want to bring a message."[4] For her, rap that promotes the early principles of peace, love, unity, and having fun is hip-hop.

Azalea's awards pointed to her success as an artist. The awards also created discomfort in the rap genre. Did her success come at the sacrifice of African-American rappers' success? Azalea has been accused of mimicking African-American English. Though the speech patterns are not authentic to her background, even scholarly linguists have commented that she speaks it fluently. Still, dialect and speech are cultural-identity markers. Faking them borders parody. Many artists share the opinion that it is okay for Azalea to rap, but they'd prefer to hear her use her native Australian accent.

For sounding more like a southern African American than a white Australian, Azalea has been accused of appropriating, or, in other words, stealing, the African-American musical form. One problem with appropriation is credit. History has shown that white musicians can get more credit than the African-American artists who influenced them. Another problem is that white artists get to promote their own careers without suffering the injustice of racism. "I don't think the voice makes me fake," said Azalea in 2016. "It makes me an artist."[5] It seems that some fans don't agree. Due to low ticket sales, she canceled some tour dates in 2016.

Despite success, Azalea has faced criticism for her African-American sound and what some consider appropriation.

8 HIP-HOP MOVES FORWARD

In some cases, artists who remain independent are freer from harsh critical attention than big-label artists. They either make it on the basis of their own merits, or they don't. There are many women creating rap music, by choice, in underground hip-hop. Coming from a broad geography and a wide demographic, these artists represent an array of musical styles.

Independent Artists

White hip-hop artist Dessa (Margret Wander) was born in Minneapolis, Minnesota, in 1981. Her highly original art has not been challenged as Iggy Azalea's has. Introduced to rap at a poetry slam, the overlap between poetry and rap inspired Dessa as a spoken-word artist. She

Minneapolis native Dessa chose an independent career path.

Dessa is the only female member of Doomtree.

joined Doomtree, an indie rap collective in Minneapolis. Its other members are all men, and most are white. She released three solo albums, sang on her fellow artists' solo albums, and appeared on Doomtree collective albums. The rapper is now the CEO of Doomtree's indie record label. She followed her debut, *A Badly Broken Code*, with *Castor, the Twin*, and mixes rap and singing with performance art.

Jean Grae has carved an enduring career as an independent artist. She has a large fan base, is considered an underground icon, and, as one reviewer said, is "one of hip-hop's most promising rappers."[1] Grae (Tsidi Ibrahim, born 1976) is a native of Cape Town, South Africa, but was raised in New York. She has collaborated on tracks with independent artists Atmosphere, the Roots, Talib Kweli, Mos Def, and Immortal Technique, to name a few. She thrives onstage.

Being an independent artist allows her the freedom to perform songs her fans have never heard before. Her solo albums, including *Attack of the Attacking Things*

> "We don't get to discuss actual artistry. Technical skill. Ninety-nine percent of the conversation is 'what is it like to be a woman MC.' It makes me terribly depressed. Your whole life as an artist goes ignored."[2]
>
> —*Jean Grae*, New Republic, *2015*

Jean Grae performs at rapper Royce Da 5'9"'s album release party in 2011.

(2002), *This Week* (2004), and *Jeanius* (2008), received high acclaim. Grae seems to have no interest in signing to bigger, commercial labels. As she says, "I don't like to play by the rules."[3] Being independent allows her to use her imagination in whichever way she chooses. She works on her own terms, rapping about her own themes. In 2014, she launched a web series, *Life with Jeannie*, which she wrote, directed, and produced. The show has a black female lead and an all-black cast.

"Hip-hop history desperately needs more women telling stories on their own terms: It's the only way to ensure we'll have an accurate record of their legacies."[4]

—*Stacia L. Brown*, New Republic *magazine*

Rapsody (Marlanna Evans) from Snow Hill, North Carolina, prolifically releases mixtapes. She is produced by the indie label It's A Wonderful World Music Group. With her soulful style, she has been compared to Lauryn Hill. In contrast, Lizzo (Melissa Jefferson, born 1988), from Minneapolis, raps like it's a race. In her song "Faded," she raps, "Don't tell us to slow it down, we won't listen / We're twenty-somethings and it's 20-something." She founded The Chalice and Grrrl Prty, which are all-girl indie hip-hop groups.

Some indie MCs demonstrate hometown loyalty. Awkwafina studied in Beijing, China, before returning to Queens, where she grew up, and breaking into rap. She creates videos of her songs in recognizable New York City locations. FM Supreme is well-known in Chicago. Addressing social themes familiar to Chicago natives, she won various poetry slams in her hometown. She has shared the stage with MCs such as Lupe Fiasco, MC Lyte, and Common.

BIOPICS OF WOMEN

Notorious, a 2009 biopic about Notorious B.I.G.'s life, minimized Lil' Kim as an MC. She was depicted as being only a love interest, not a rapper in her own right. In 2010, BET screened a documentary called "My Mic Sounds Nice: The Truth About Women in Hip Hop," directed by Ava DuVernay, the first African-American woman to direct a $100-million feature film.[5] Fans of hip-hop are anticipating films about the major female MCs. Many legendary figures from hip-hop's early periods still work actively in the hip-hop community. Though not all of them are still performing, many are fulfilling hip-hop's mission to improve the lives of children and teens.

Broadening Hip-Hop

Independent artists have broadened the scope of what a woman can do in the hip-hop world. They illustrate ways in which hip-hop has survived and thrived, and how it continues to change. The culture is now old enough to have historical periods. Hip-hop Studies is emerging as a growing academic presence. Critics and scholars are analyzing its evolution from its earliest era.

The 2015 film *Straight Outta Compton*, the story of N.W.A's breakout success, was a box office hit. *The Get Down*, a 2016 Netflix Original series, tells a fictionalized version of hip-hop's first moments with DJ Kool Herc and Grandmaster Flash. It contains historically accurate details in its script, setting, and costumes. Films of hip-hop's history are bringing new attention to the genre. However, some "best of" lists include no female MCs. Whole articles about rap history make no mention of the women of hip-hop. Hip-hop historians are still trying to determine how, where, and even if women fit into the genre. Audiences are wondering when biopic films will be

EARLY HIP-HOP FILMS

In 1983, Lisa Lee was the only woman rapper in the film *Wild Style*, a local project about early hip-hop culture. "It turned out to be history," Lisa Lee said. "It was an amazing thing years later to see what we did as children."[6] *Beat Street*, filmed in 1984 and set in the South Bronx, told a story of teens immersed in hip-hop. MCs Debbie D, Sha Rock, and Lisa Lee make brief appearances. That same year, *Style Wars* documented New York City's graffiti art. The three films capture the historic hip-hop era. More than a decade later, in 1999, filmmaker Rachel Raimist directed *Nobody Knows My Name*, the first documentary about women in hip-hop. Raimist featured talented artists working in hip-hop and struggling to be heard in the community.

MC Lyte was one of the founding feminists of hip-hop and is also in demand as a DJ.

made of influential female rap stars.

When hip-hop women bring their talents to the eclectic hip-hop mix, their contributions do not end. Women continue to preserve hip-hop culture and keep it relevant today by inspiring others. Whenever new artists come up, the influence of women of the past helps them reinvent the art form.

HIP-HOP IN THE WHITE HOUSE

In October 2015, President Barack Obama and First Lady Michelle held an event called "In Performance at the White House: A Celebration of American Creativity." Among the talented guests were two rappers. In honor of her HBO biopic film *Bessie*, about singer Bessie Smith, Queen Latifah performed "Preachin' The Blues." MC Lyte represented hip-hop culture with her songs "Dear John" and "Cha Cha Cha."

TIMELINE

1979

With Sylvia Robinson producing, the Sugarhill Gang records "Rapper's Delight."

1981

MC Sha Rock, with Funky 4+1, perform on national television, appearing on *Saturday Night Live*.

1983

The film *Wild Style* captures early hip-hop culture. Lisa Lee is the only female rapper featured.

1984

Responding to UTFO's "Roxanne Roxanne," Roxanne Shanté makes rap's first recorded diss song, "Roxanne's Revenge."

1986

Salt-N-Pepa drops *Hot, Cool & Vicious*.

1989

J. J. Fad becomes the first all-female posse to earn a Grammy nomination for Best Rap Performance for the song "Supersonic"; Queen Latifah drops *All Hail the Queen*.

1996

Lil' Kim's X-rated solo album, *Hard Core*, goes double platinum.

1997

Missy Elliott drops *Supa Dupa Fly*.

1998

Lauryn Hill releases *The Miseducation of Lauryn Hill.*

1999

Lauryn Hill wins five Grammy Awards for *The Miseducation of Lauryn Hill*, including Album of the Year; in September, Eve debuts *Let There Be Eve...Ruff Ryders' First Lady*. She is the third female MC, after Lauryn Hill and Foxy Brown, to have a number one album.

2003

Fergie adds strong vocals to the Black Eyed Peas' "Where Is the Love?," bringing rap and pop together for a social commentary after the September 11, 2001, terrorist attacks.

2008

Nicki Minaj wins Female Artist of the Year at the Underground Music Awards.

2012

Angel Haze's mixtape *Classick* includes the song "Cleaning Out My Closet," which tells the horrors of being sexually abused as a child.

2015

In October, Queen Latifah and MC Lyte perform for President and First Lady Obama in the White House.

ESSENTIAL
FACTS

OLD SCHOOL 1973–1984

Sha Rock becomes an original member of the Funky 4+1. Sylvia Robinson founds hip-hop's first production company, Sugar Hill Records.

NEW SCHOOL 1984–1990

Queen Latifah is one of hip-hop's first solo MCs. She inspires MC Lyte and many others. Her songs, such as "Ladies First" and "U.N.I.T.Y.," are called game changers.

GOLDEN ERA

Salt-N-Pepa breaks boundaries with songs such as "Push It" and "Let's Talk About Sex." Starting with *Supa Dupa Fly*, Missy Elliott's career soars. She is called one of the best rappers of all time.

GANGSTA RAP

After producing J. J. Fad's "Supersonic," N.W.A drops *Straight Outta Compton*, fueling gangsta rap. Yo-Yo proves to rap as tough as Ice Cube, one of N.W.A's male MCs. Rappers such as Lil' Kim and Foxy Brown represent this era with provocative lyrics and frank sexuality.

NEW MILLENNIUM

Nicki Minaj achieves enormous popularity.

INDIE AND UNDERGROUND ARTISTS

Artists such as Jean Grae and Angel Haze work with independent labels or offer their mixtapes for free online.

KEY QUOTES

"Women have always been a presence in male-founded hip-hop groups. . . . The woman is either the hypersexualized mascot or the secret-weapon anomaly that proves—surprise!—girls can rap, too."

—Janelle Harris, Atlantic *magazine, 2016*

"I want to be seen as a hardworking businesswoman who really takes pride in writing and rapping in a way that still shows that I'm hungry. I'm still hip-hop—and that's never going to change. But I do know that I've worked really, really hard to perfect my craft and give people something that I can be proud of."

—Nicki Minaj, Vogue, *2015*

"Hip-hop history desperately needs more women telling stories on their own terms: It's the only way to ensure we'll have an accurate record of their legacies."

—Stacia L. Brown, New Republic *magazine*

GLOSSARY

B-GIRL
Short for break-girl, a break dance performer.

BIOPIC
A biographical film.

CAMEO
A small but noticeable appearance of a celebrity in a film, play, song, or other art form.

COMMERCIAL
Viewed with a regard for profit.

DISS
Short for *disrespect*; to criticize someone or something.

DJ
Disc jockey; the artist who plays the beats and background music in rap songs.

DOPE
Cool.

FREESTYLE
Improvisational; making up lyrics on the spot, often in performance and sometimes in response to a challenge.

GANGSTA RAP
A type of rap music with lyrics featuring the violence and drug use of urban gang life.

MAINSTREAM

A dominant trend in art or music, widely known and accepted as conventional.

MC

A person who speaks over a beat; interchangeable with "rapper."

MISOGYNY

Hatred of or contempt for women.

PANSEXUAL

Not limited in sexual choice with regard to biological sex, gender, or gender identity.

SAMPLE

To borrow short sections of previously recorded songs and use them as the background of a new song, sometimes repeatedly.

SCRATCHING

Moving a record back and forth under the needle to create a beat.

SUBCULTURE

A small culture with interests and beliefs that are new or different from the larger culture or society.

TAG

A graffiti writer's signature, the most basic form of graffiti, or the act of signing one's tag.

ADDITIONAL RESOURCES

SELECTED BIBLIOGRAPHY

Bradley, Adam, and Andrew DuBois. *The Anthology of Rap*. New Haven, CT: Yale UP, 2010. Print.

Charnas, Dan. *The Big Payback: The History of the Business of Hip-Hop*. New York: New American Library, 2010. Print.

Edwards, Paul. *The Concise Guide to Hip-Hop Music*. New York: St. Martin's Griffin, 2015. Print.

FURTHER READINGS

Berlatsky, Noah, ed. *Rap Music: Introducing Issues with Opposing Viewpoints*. Farmington Hills, MI: Greenhaven, 2013. Print.

Pough, Gwendolyn D. *Home Girls Make Some Noise: Hip-Hop Feminism Anthology*. New York: Parker, 2007. Print.

WEBSITES

To learn more about Hip-Hop Insider, visit **abdobooklinks.com**. These links are routinely monitored and updated to provide the most current information available.

FOR MORE INFORMATION

For more information on this subject, contact or visit the following organizations:

HUSH TOURS, INC.
Church St. Station PO BOX 2319
New York, NY 10008
212-714-3544
http://www.hushtours.com/
Choose from six hip-hop tours through the Bronx, Harlem, and Brooklyn. Bus tours are led by hip-hop legends such as Grandmaster Caz, Kurtis Blow, and DJ Kool Herc.

UNIVERSAL HIP HOP MUSEUM
555 Bergen Avenue, 3rd Floor
New York, NY 10452
347-454-2793
http://www.uhhm.org/
Education programs, virtual exhibits, digital collections, and more are available for experiencing at the Universal Hip Hop Museum.

SOURCE NOTES

CHAPTER 1. LAURYN HILL'S NIGHT

1. Latifah Muhammad. "Making 'The Score': A Look at the Fugees' Final Album with the Producers." *Vibe*. Vibe, 16 Feb. 2016. Web. 10 Oct. 2016.

2. Leah Furman and Elina Furman. *Heart of Soul: The Lauryn Hill Story.* Topeka, KS: Topeka Bindery, 1999. Print. 128–129.

3. Laura Checkoway. "Inside *The Miseducation of Lauryn Hill.*" *Rolling Stone*. Rolling Stone, 26 Aug. 2008. Web. 9 Oct. 2016.

4. Christopher John Farley. "Songs in the Key of Lauryn Hill." *Time* 152.10 (1998): 72. *EBSCOhost*. 30 Sept. 2016.

5. Tom Barnes. "Nearly 20 Years Ago, Lauryn Hill Made an Album So Perfectly It Nearly Ruined Her Life." *Music.Mic*. Mic Network, 25 Aug. 2015. Web. 29 Sept. 2016.

CHAPTER 2. FOUNDERS OF HIP-HOP

1. "Peace, Unity, Love, and Having Fun." *ScannersInc*. ScannersInc, 12 July 2014. Web. 28 Sept. 2016.

2. "Lady Pink." *Brooklyn Museum*. Brooklyn Museum, n.d. Web. 11 Oct. 2016.

3. Michael Friedman. "Why MC Sha Rock Is Still the Luminary Icon." *Psychology Today*. Psychology Today, 1 June 2016. Web. 23 Oct. 2016.

4. Callum McGeoch. "Sylvia Robinson: Rapper's Delight." *Dazed*. Dazed, n.d. Web. 17 Oct. 2016.

5. Dan Charnas. *The Big Payback: The History of the Business of Hip-Hop*. New York: New American Library, 2010. Print. 43.

6. "Mercedes Ladies." *Old School Hip Hop*. Old School Hip Hop, 7 Jan. 2010. Web. 17 Sept. 2016.

7. "Lady B." *Old School Hip Hop*. Old School Hip Hop, 12 Aug. 2010. Web. 17 Sept. 2016.

CHAPTER 3. STANDING OUT

1. Erik Ross. "The 50 Best Selling Rap Albums of All Time." *Complex*. Complex Media, 18 May 2013. Web. 21 Sept. 2016.

2. Sarah Oakes. "Why Salt-N-Pepa Were 20 Years Ahead of Their Time." *Daily Life*. Fairfax Media, 6 Apr. 2015. Web. 20 Sept. 2016.

3. Queen Latifah and Karen Hunter. *Ladies First: The Revelations of a Strong Woman*. New York: William Morrow, 1999. Print. 38.

4. D.E. Thigpen. "Not For Men Only." *Time* 137.21 (1991): 71. *MasterFILE Premier*. Web. 15 Nov. 2016.

5. MC Lyte. "MC Lyte Explains How to Join the Recording Academy and Vote in the Grammy Awards." *HipHopDX*. HipHopDX, 13 Jan. 2015. Web. 16 Sept. 2016.

CHAPTER 4. CHANGING IMAGES FOR WOMEN

1. "Oprah Talks to Sean Combs." *Oprah.com*. Harpo Productions, n.d. Web. 19 Sept. 2016.

2. Yolanda "Yoyo" Whitaker. "Reclaiming The Mike." *Essence* 36.6 (2005): 136. *MasterFILE Premier*. Web. 15 Nov. 2016.

3. Neva Chonin. "Da Brat: Unrestricted." *Rolling Stone*. Rolling Stone, 11 May 2000. Web. 16 Sept. 2016.

4. Ronda Racha Penrice. "Unsung on Rapper YoYo: 25 Years Later, You Still Can't Play Her Out." *The Root*. The Root, 16 Sept 2015. Web. 16 Sept. 2016.

5. Janelle Harris. "The Radical Power of 'Killing Me Softly.'" *Atlantic*. Atlantic Monthly Group, 1 June 2016. Web. 17 Sept. 2016.

6. Erika Ramirez. "Ladies First: 31 Female Rappers Who Changed Hip-Hop." *Billboard*. Billboard, 31 Mar. 2014. Web. 17 Sept. 2016.

7. Rob Marriott. "What Price Queen Bee?" *Hip-Hop Divas*. New York: Three Rivers, 2001. Print. 133–134.

8. Sidney Madden. "Today in Hip-Hop: Eve Drops 'Let There Be Eve… Ruff Ryders' First Lady' Album." *XXL*. XXL Network, 14 Sept. 2016. Web. 21 Sept. 2016.

9. Eeshé White. "Eve on Female Rappers Going to Jail: 'I'm Glad They're All Out.'" *Boombox*. XXL Network, 19 Apr. 2016. Web. 19 Sept. 2016.

CHAPTER 5. WOMEN IN CHARGE

1. Hilton Als. "The New Negro." *New Yorker*. Condé Nast, 20 Oct. 1997. Web. 20 Sept. 2016.

CHAPTER 6. RAP, POP, AND WOMEN

1. Katie Sharp. "The Black Eyed Peas Are One of Music's Greatest Tragedies." *Music.Mic*. Mic Network, 23 Oct. 2014. Web. 9 Sept. 2016.

2. Bianca Sepulveda. "Feminists Call for Hip-hop Reform." *University of Chicago Magazine* 97.5 (2005). Web. 10 Sept. 2016.

3. "Hip Hop Gurlz." *YouTube*. YouTube, 17 Feb. 2014. Web. 17 Sept. 2016.

4. "The Issues." *Independent Lens*. Independent Television Service, n.d. Web. 9 Sept. 2016.

5. "Oprah Talks to Sean Combs." *Oprah.com*. Harpo Productions, n.d. Web. 19 Sept. 2016.

6. Lisa Robinson. "Rihanna in Cuba: The Cover Story." *Vanity Fair*. Condé Nast, 6 Oct 2015. Web. 10 Oct. 2016.

SOURCE NOTES
CONTINUED

CHAPTER 7. MAINSTREAM AND INDIE STARS

1. Alex Frank. "Newly Single Nicki Minaj on Feminism, Meek Mill, and Rapping at 50." *Vogue*. Vogue, 12 Feb. 2015. Web. 25 Sept. 2016.

2. Ibid.

3. Jeff Guo. "How Iggy Azalea Mastered Her 'Blaccent.'" *Washington Post*. Washington Post, 4 Jan. 2016. Web. 9 Sept. 2016.

4. Lauren Schwartzberg. "Hip-Hop's First Female MCs Approve of Iggy Azalea." *Vice*. Vice, 19 Aug. 2014. Web. 10 Oct. 2016.

5. Jeff Guo. "How Iggy Azalea Mastered Her 'Blaccent.'" *Washington Post*. Washington Post, 4 Jan. 2016. Web. 9 Sept. 2016.

CHAPTER 8. HIP-HOP MOVES FORWARD

1. Jamin Warren. "Jean Grae: This Week." *Pitchfork*. Pitchfork, 4 Oct. 2004. Web. 7 Sept. 2016.

2. Stacia L. Brown. "It's Time to Tell the Stories of Women in Hip-hop." *New Republic*. New Republic, 26 Aug. 2015. Web. 17 Sept. 2016.

3. Nathan Leigh. "Underground Hip-Hop Icon Jean Grae Talks Activism, Education in South Africa." *AFROPUNK*. AFROPUNK, 29 Jan. 2014. Web. 18 Sept. 2016.

4. Stacia L. Brown. "It's Time to Tell the Stories of Women in Hip-hop." *New Republic*. New Republic, 26 Aug. 2015. Web. 17 Sept. 2016.

5. Yohana Desta. "Ava Du Vernay Is First Black Female Director to Helm a $100 Million Film." *Vanity Fair*. Vanity Fair, 4 Aug. 2016. Web. 4 Oct. 2016.

6. Lauren Schwartzberg. "Hip-Hop's First Female MCs Approve of Iggy Azalea." *Vice*. Vice, 19 Aug. 2014. Web. 10 Oct. 2016.

INDEX

ABOUT THE AUTHOR

Sheila Llanas has an MFA in poetry. She taught at the Johns Hopkins Center for Talented Youth (CTY) and the University of Wisconsin–Waukesha. She has authored more than 40 nonfiction books for children and teens, including the Essential Lives title *Jonas Salk: Medical Innovator and Polio Vaccine Developer* and the Essential Critiques title *How to Analyze the Works of Suzanne Collins*.